NARLA AND THE HIDDEN TREASURE

Lisa Domeny

This book is dedicated to Narla, Buffy and Mr Banks. Despite their outward appearance, these three dogs discovered their inner beauty with the help of a loving family.

It is also dedicated to anyone who has ever felt 'less than'. May we all learn to discover our own HIDDEN TREASURE, our own uniqueness, celebrate it and share it with the world.

Lisa Domeny

www.facebook.com/pages/Team-Golden-Oldies/1410374712576426

© 2015 by Lisa Domeny.
All rights reserved.

Team Golden Oldies™
Pet Publishing Plus

ISBN-13: 978-0-9943239-1-0

FRIENDS FOREVER

The need is great for adopting senior dogs all over the world. Despite the wonderful characteristics of wisdom, loyalty and unconditional love, these dogs are often overlooked for younger versions of themselves.

Narla and 12 year old rescue dog Buffy became the best of friends through the TEAM GOLDEN OLDIES Facebook page. Although they had very hard lives, both proved that beauty does indeed comes from within. Narla and Buffy lived every day with gratitude and infinite love for the people around them.

The common passion of loving senior dogs extends not just on Earth but to the moon and back...

Leigh Ann Combs

Hi my name is Narla and I am an old rescue dog.

Will you be my friend?

Before I was adopted I was all alone.

My fur coat was yucky and
full of fleas so it had to be shaved off.

I was really worried that when I arrived in my new home that I wouldn't make friends.

How could anyone love me looking like this?

This made me feel sad and lonely.

So I decided I would think of ways to make people love me and be my friend.

Maybe if I was a pirate I would make new friends?

Maybe if I changed my hairstyle I would make new friends?

Maybe if I covered my face with soot
I would make new friends?

Maybe if I wore funny hats I would make new friends?

Maybe if I wore flowers in my hair
I would make new friends?

Maybe, just maybe, if I rolled in kangaroo poo,
I would make new friends?

WARNING! - Rolling in kangaroo poo DOES NOT
make you new friends! It only means you have to have a bath.

One day mum asked me why I was trying to change the way I looked.

I told her, "So people will like me and be my friend."

"But Narla," Mum said "It doesn't matter what's on the outside. It's what's in your heart that matters.

As long as you have love in your heart, you will always make friends. It's like a hidden treasure chest and only YOU have the key to open it."

"Love in my heart", I have LOTS of love in my heart!

This thought made me feel VERY, VERY happy!

So I decided to show people my hidden treasure, the love in my heart and share that love with everyone I met.

As a therapy dog I visited the nursing home and made people smile and be happy.

I made friends with the residents Stella, Wyn and even staff member Cathy.

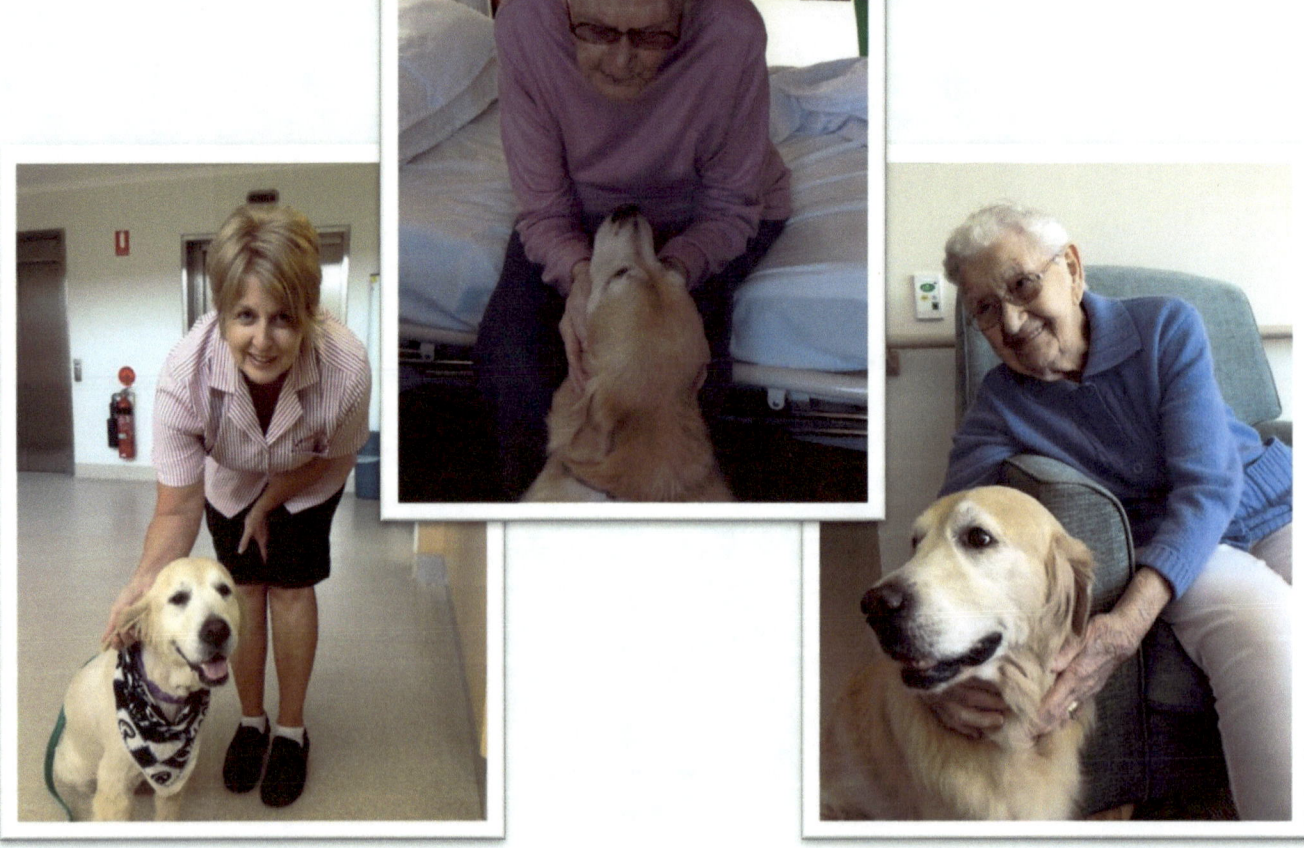

I went to the park and gave out free hugs and made friends with Kyana.

I went to the ANZAC Day March and supported the troops with my brother Winnie and sister Zoe, and made friends with the other supporters in the crowd.

I made friends with Jared as he pulled me and Winnie around in Winnie's Red WINNIEbago.

I made friends with Cec and Lois as I visited them each week in their home.

Lois makes the best morning tea for mum and gives us lots of treats and cuddles.

I made friends with Dr Shae, our vet, when we visited her each week for our cuddles when we get weighed.

I even made friends with Nat, the Hairiest Postman in Australia, if not THE WORLD, as he delivered our mail.

As I looked at all my new friends I realised what
mum had told me WAS true.

The love in my heart IS like a hidden treasure.
But it is a very special treasure because
it grows in value when you share it with others.

Today my hidden treasure is no longer hidden. Just like a jewelled crown, it is shining bright for all to see.

I hope each of you will seek and find your own hidden treasure and share it with others.

When you do, remember it was an old rescue dog named Narla who told you where to look and find it.

Love and licks
Your friend Narla.

MORE FROM THIS AUTHOR

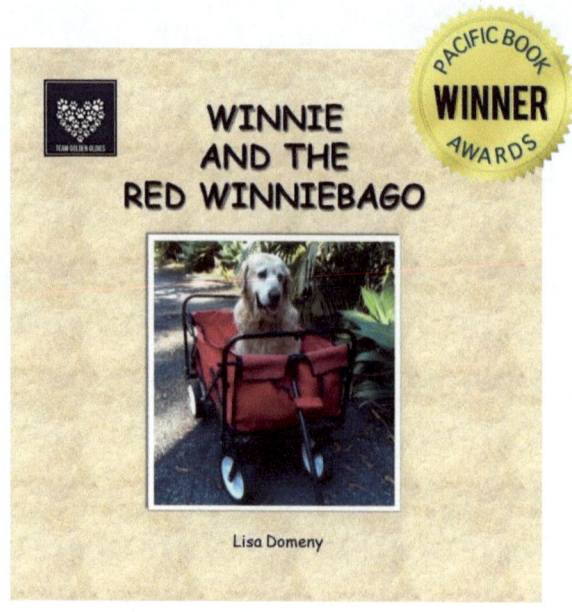

Winnie and the Red Winniebago

Winnie the senior rescue dog's mission to spread kindness and love is challenged when he can no longer walk. Determined to continue his adventures, Winnie's family and friends find a way for him to keep spreading love and happiness to the world!

In sharing her love of old rescue dogs and their adventures, Lisa Domeny has provided a beautiful, positive and uplifting story for children to learn about overcoming life's challenges, friendship and spreading kindness and love to make the world a better place.

 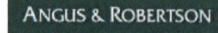

Team Golden Oldies Store
www.TeamGoldenOldies.com

Notes for Parents, Caregivers and Teachers

Today we know more than ever about how children learn to develop self-esteem. Children are not born with self-esteem. It is dependent on the adult carer's capacity to role model self-love and to teach each child that they have their own inherent value or (Hidden Treasure).

Each child is unique. Teaching children to value their differences helps them to realise that they are valued and don't have to look or behave like others to feel that self-worth. This helps children to learn they don't have to pretend to be something outside of their own uniqueness just to feel loved or valued. If this is not learned in the early years an unhealthy sense of competition may lead to anxiety.

Knowing one's own self-worth leads to having confidence and with each successful experience a child gains more confidence. A child's healthy emotional foundation is dependent on adults in their lives helping them to learn life skills and deal with their emotions.
One way to teach life skills is through books. Children love books and especially love having stories read to them out aloud. Reading stories each day helps children learn to cope with and learn about their feelings.

With positive self-worth, children are more likely to become adults who are accepting and tolerant of others and of their own capabilities and limitations. A child then creates self-calmness and contentment and is able to receive love from others.

Just like Narla, children come to realise that it is their own hidden treasure of love and not their outward appearance that makes them truly lovable and able to share that love with many others.

Once again Lisa Domeny, in sharing her love of old rescue dogs has gifted children with a beautiful, positive and uplifting story for young children to learn endless topics and life skills which helps build resilience in life's journey.

As a Child Health Nurse I am constantly looking for ways to share with parents the concepts of self-esteem and self-love. This book provides beautiful analogies of how we learn to love ourselves and others as well as to receive love through everyday situations and interactions. I would highly recommend it as a valuable teaching resource and the perfect companion to "Winnie and the Red Winniebago" as the perfect bedtime story for your child.

I believe Narla will indeed make many friends, and most importantly she will make the kind of friends that will find their own "hidden treasure of love," and then keep on sharing it with others.

Kim Hadley RN, RM, CA&FHN

www.ingramcontent.com/pod-product-compliance
Lightning Source LLC
Chambersburg PA
CBHW041539040426
42446CB00002B/158